The Power of
The A2s

The Power of
The A2s

Gavin Morrison

An imprint of
Ian Allan Publishing

Half title:
Heaton's very well cleaned 'A2/3' No 60511 *Airborne* makes an impressive sight at it leaves Newcastle at the head of the 3.30pm express to Birmingham New Street on 9 April 1960. *I. S. Carr*

Frontispiece:
The 10.10am King's Cross–Glasgow Queen Street, sometimes known as the 'Junior Scotsman', was one of the heaviest East Coast expresses and in the mid-1950s was entrusted to New England's 'A2/2s'. *Mons Meg* is working hard as it blasts out of Copenhagen Tunnel on its way north. *Brian Morrison*

Title page:
'A2' No 525 *A. H. Peppercorn* when new, in December 1947. *Ian Allan Library*

Below:
In 1959 *Earl Marischal* passes Penshaw with a short (five-coach) express diverted via the Leamside line. *I. S. Carr*

Bibliography

Railway Correspondence & Travel Society,
Locomotives of the LNER Parts 2A and 6B
Yeadon's *Register of LNER Locomotives* Volumes 1 and 9.

First published 2004

ISBN 0 86093 588 4

© Ian Allan Publishing Ltd 2004

Published by Oxford Publishing Co

an imprint of Ian Allan Publishing Ltd, Hersham, Surrey KT12 4RG.
Printed by Ian Allan Printing Ltd, Hersham, Surrey KT12 4RG.

Code: 0409/B

Introduction

Unlike the other Pacific classes on the East Coast main line, namely the 'A1s', 'A3s' and 'A4s', wherein there were only minor differences between locomotives, the 'A2' variations were very much more complex, involving two Chief Mechanical Engineers (Edward Thompson and A. H. Peppercorn), with Sir Nigel Gresley designing the 'P2s' from which ultimately emerged the rebuilt 'A2/2s'.

It was the wish of both author and publisher to include a short section on the 'P2s', which would otherwise be impossible to cover in a book of this format.

The 153-mile Edinburgh–Aberdeen route was extremely difficult to work, with steep gradients in awkward places, notably at Dundee, and very sharp curves. Gresley had never been enthusiastic about double-heading anywhere, and, as Pacifics were not allowed to be double-headed on this line, he set about sorting the problems with an extremely powerful 2-8-2 (Mikado), capable of hauling trains in excess of 500 tons on the line. First drawings appeared at the end of March 1932 at Doncaster, culminating in the completion of No 2001 *Cock o' the North* in May 1934. The result was considered by some to be the most impressive locomotive to be built in this country up to this time. No 2001 was the first locomotive by Gresley to be fitted with Kylchap double blastpipe and chimney. Extensive trials were carried out on

Above:
'P2/1' No 2001 *Cock o' the North* as originally built.
Ian Allan Library

Below:
'P2/2' No 2001 *Cock o' the North* as rebuilt with
streamlined casing. *Ian Allan Library*

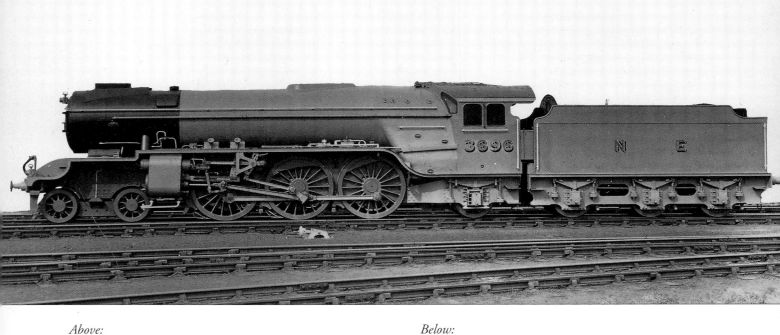

Above:
'A2/1' No 3696 as turned out in May 1944 in photographic grey, as yet unnamed and with 'V2' tender. *Ian Allan Library*

Below:
'A2/2' No 60506 *Wolf of Badenoch* at Grantham shed, 18 June 1955. *J. P. Wilson / Rail Archive Stephenson*

Above:
The 'A2/1s' were regular performers on the Waverley route.
On 14 June 1958 *Highland Chieftain* was in charge of the
down 'Waverley' express from London St Pancras to
Edinburgh and is seen approaching Newcastleton. *R. Leslie*

the south end of the East Coast main line, resulting in
many alterations to assist steaming, including a two-month
visit to the SNCF testing plant at Vitry-sur-Seine, near
Paris. In October 1934 No 2001 was sent to Haymarket to
work the Aberdeen trains and soon gained the reputation
for being the miners' friend; indeed, during early testing
it ran out of coal at Dalmeny on the return leg of an
Edinburgh–Dundee working. In their early days the 'P2s'
were not allowed to work all the way to Aberdeen for fear
of running out of coal, so their efficiency in terms of
diagramming was somewhat reduced, as engines had to be
changed at Dundee. There were, however, no doubts about
their ability to haul heavy trains, as they steamed well
(albeit at the expense of the fireman) and rode well, but
they suffered from damaged crank axles as a result of
overheating big-ends (attributed to the curvature of the
Edinburgh–Aberdeen line) — a problem which was never
really solved and which may have ultimately persuaded
Edward Thompson to rebuild them as Class A2/2s. The six
locomotives varied considerably from each other, brief
details being given in the photo captions, but for a more
detailed explanation the reader can do no better than refer
to Part 6B of the Railway Correspondence & Travel Society
book *Locomotives of the LNER*.

After Sir Nigel Gresley's death in April 1941 his
successor, Edward Thompson, lost little time in producing
drawings for rebuilding the 'P2s' as 'A2/2' Pacifics.
No 2005 *Thane of Fife* was selected first and duly appeared
in 1943 as a very much more austere-looking locomotive,
with greater emphasis on ease of maintenance, this being

no surprise during wartime. All the rebuilds returned to
Scotland and the Aberdeen route but achieved poor
mileage between general repairs. It was suggested that the
standard of maintenance at Cowlairs Works was at the root
of the problem, so in 1949 all were transferred south, their
allocation split equally between York and New England
depots, where they remained, somewhat in the
background, until withdrawal. An interesting statistic is
that 'A2/2' *Wolf of Badenoch* was shopped 30 times between
1945 and 1959, whereas 'A1'/'A3' *Flying Scotsman* made
just 11 visits over the same period, and the fact that the
'A2/2s' achieved relatively low mileages probably says it all
about the success or otherwise of their rebuilding.

Unlike all other 'A2' variants the four 'A2/1s' were
constructed at Darlington, where they had been started as
'V2s', and the type was effectively a Pacific version of the
Gresley design, with many modifications. The 'V'-shaped
cab was retained, as were the six-wheeled tender and the
boiler, although the latter's pressure was increased to
225lb/sq in. Trials took place with No 3697 in January
1945 against 'A2/2' No 2003 *Lord President* and 'A4'
No 2512 *Silver Fox* but appeared to be beset with
problems. Fresh trials were conducted in May 1945

Above:
'A2/3' No 60512 *Steady Aim* in the yard at York shed,
13 May 1962. *Gavin Morrison*

Right:
On a very wet 30 May 1958 *Sayajirao* pauses at Hawick
with a humble all-stations to Carlisle. The Haymarket
Pacifics were regular performers on passenger workings over
the Waverley route. Note the very tall signalbox (in the
background) and the wooden platform surface. All traces of
the station have since vanished, and the Teviot leisure
centre now occupies the site. *T. G. Hepburn /
Rail Archive Stephenson*

whereby 18-coach trains were hauled with ease between
King's Cross and Grantham, and a maximum of 758 tons
of freight. The locomotive handled these tasks with ease,
but the 'V2' tender was considered unsuitable. *Duke of
Rothesay* aside, the 'A2/1s' spent most of their time in
Scotland; although never in the limelight at Haymarket,
they could be seen on a variety of routes and workings,
including the principal named Scottish expresses, as
illustrated in the book, but were seen south of Newcastle
only when *en route* to or from Doncaster Works.

The emergence of the first of 15 'A2/3s' — No 500
Edward Thompson — in LNER apple green from Doncaster
Works in May 1946 was notable in that this was the first
new Pacific turned out by the 'Plant' for eight years. Along
with the second example — No 511 *Airborne* — it was
used at first on local passenger workings to iron out the
initial problems. Tests were conducted to compare No 500
with 'V2' 2-6-2 No 959 between Newcastle and Edinburgh
with 459 tons, resulting in significantly heavier coal
consumption by the 'A2/3'. The tests revealed many
problems, but it was clear that the 'A2/3' could easily have
hauled a heavier load than could the 'V2'. Allocation of the
sub-class was initially shared between the Eastern and
North Eastern Regions, with the exception of No 60519
Honeyway, which spent all its days on the Scottish Region.
The locomotives were to be seen heading a wide variety of
workings the whole length of the East Coast main line,
including Leeds, and (especially when new) could be seen
on the best-known trains, but gradually, as the 'A3s' and
'A4s' were sorted out after the war and the Peppercorn 'A1s'
appeared on the scene, the 'A2s' tended to be relegated to
less glamorous work. Although these locomotives were
perfectly capable of working anything in the timetables, few
timing logs seem to be available showing their exploits,
although No 60524 *Herringbone* (it is claimed) made one

of the fastest start-to-stop runs between York and
Darlington with a heavy load; no doubt the magic 100mph
was achieved down Stoke Bank on some unrecorded
occasion. Two members of the class finished their days as
replacements for ex-LMS 'Princess Coronation' Pacifics at
Glasgow's Polmadie shed (where they met with little
enthusiasm from crews), the rest being withdrawn after
short working lives due to the arrival of diesel-electrics.

The Peppercorn 'A2s', all save No 60539 were built with
single chimneys, and will always be mainly associated with
Scotland, especially the Aberdeen route from Edinburgh.
Beauty is in the eyes of the beholder (or so it is said), and
in the author's opinion a single-chimney 'A2' in LNER
apple or BR Brunswick green was the finest-looking Pacific
ever to run in this country; it is a pity that initial steaming
problems seemed to be solved by altering some of them to
the Kylchap double chimney. After much experimenting,
both officially and unofficially, by the Scottish sheds,

especially Haymarket, the single-chimney locomotives performed reasonably well, albeit nowhere near as well as the two double-chimney examples — Nos 60532 *Blue Peter* and 60529 *Pearl Diver* — allocated to Scotland. With the exception of No 60529 (sent to Haymarket), the Peppercorn 'A2s' were allocated initially to Eastern and North Eastern sheds, working all the principal expresses. In the summer of 1949, however, five were sent to Scotland because of the poor performance of the 'A2/2s', and in November it was decided to exchange the 'A2/2s' in Scotland for 'A2s' on a permanent basis, after which Scotland had 11 'A2s', the NER three, and the ER one (No 60533 at New England), which situation pertained until withdrawal. All the North Eastern locomotives were fitted with double chimneys and multiple-valve regulators. The Scottish ones were shared between Aberdeen Ferryhill, Dundee and Haymarket and were mainly employed on the Aberdeen route. In 1963, by which time there was little work left in the east of Scotland, Nos 60527/30/5 joined the two 'A2/3s' in moving to Glasgow Polmadie as replacements for 'Princess Coronations' but did little work there. The end for the class came in December 1966, when Nos 60530 and 60532 were withdrawn, the Scottish locomotives having outlasted their English cousins by around three years.

No 60532 *Blue Peter* was stored for a year at Thornton shed and on 29 March 1968 was sold to Messrs G. S. Drury and J. B. Hollingsworth. In August it moved to York, where it remained until May 1970, thereafter moving to Neville Hill and, in May 1972, to Didcot; other storage locations included Walton Colliery (near Wakefield) and Dinting. By this time it had been restored to working order in apple-green livery, complete with historically inaccurate number 532 and 'L N E R' on the tender. The locomotive was later transferred to ICI Wilton, where restoration to main-line condition began in 1986, this being completed at the North Yorkshire Moors Railway after a long-term loan agreement had been reached with the North Eastern Locomotive Preservation Group (NELPG). Having emerged in 1991 in Brunswick green as BR 60532, it entered main-line service in 1992, visiting locations as diverse as Plymouth, Holyhead, Glasgow and Aberdeen, and produced some sparkling performances. It is now on display at the DarlingtonRailway Museum, awaiting a major overhaul. Readers wishing to join the NELPG should contact the Membership Secretary, Mr C. Smith, 32 Woodlea, Houghton-le-Spring, Tyne & Wear, DH5 8HT.

This book — believed to be the first in hardback solely devoted to the 'A2s' — is an attempt to show the various sub-classes in all their livery changes and major visual modifications, and to cover the areas and workings of the locomotives. As always this would not have been possible without the help of all the photographers whose work appears in the album and to whom I extend my grateful thanks.

Gavin Morrison
Mirfield
March 2004

Above:
An impressive picture of No 2001 *Cock o' the North*, taken at Doncaster Works in May 1934, clearly showing the double chimney; No 2001 was the first LNER locomotive to have the Kylchap double blastpipe and was also fitted with Lentz rotary-cam poppet valvegear and an ACFI feed-water heater. *Ian Allan Library*

Right:
Cock o' the North was allocated new to Doncaster, where a close eye could be kept on it by the works during its trial runs on the southern half of the East Coast main line. This picture shows the locomotive on test at Grantham during its first few weeks.
A. C. Cawston

Below:
Cock o' the North was much in demand in this country to attend exhibitions, but in November 1934 it was sent to the locomotive-testing station at Vitry-sur-Seine, near Paris, travelling by sea from Parkeston Quay. It is seen following arrival in France, surrounded by SNCF locomotives.
O. V. S. Bulleid

Left:
Another view of *Cock o' the North* in France, this time at Amiens station.
O. V. S. Bulleid

Below left:
Between 11 and 16 June 1934 and again on the 18th *Cock o' the North* was used to work the 10.50am King's Cross–Peterborough, returning on the 2.48pm to King's Cross. This picture was probably taken on one of these days and shows it near Brookman's Park. *C. Stevens*

Below:
Cock o' the North captured crossing the Royal Border Bridge at Berwick-upon-Tweed, returning to Haymarket shed on 22 August 1939 after a general overhaul at Doncaster. As a 'P2' the locomotive covered 362,136 miles (125,670 prior to rebuilding with piston valves), giving it an average of around 35,000 per annum — quite high, considering the time spent in testing, visiting France etc and its 20 works visits, which included eight heavy and general overhauls. *E. R. Wethersett*

Above:
During its third general overhaul at Doncaster (between 30 September 1937 and April 1938) *Cock o' the North* was rebuilt and streamlined and fitted with standard piston valvegear. It is seen in this condition at an unidentified shed on 11 August 1946. *Ian Allan Library*

Left:
No 2002 *Earl Marischal* emerged from Doncaster Works nearly six months after *Cock o' the North*, fitted with piston valves and Walschaerts/Gresley valvegear. Coal consumption, while still high, was considered to be lower than that for the earlier locomotive, and the feed-water heater was not fitted. However, smoke drifting became a problem, owing to the softer beat compared to the poppet-valve *Cock o' the North*, requiring the fitting of large outer smoke-deflectors, clearly visible in this picture of *Earl Marischal* on an up express at Peterborough late in 1934 or early in 1935. *E. Woods*

Below:
No details exist about this picture, but it again clearly shows the smoke-deflectors. *Ian Allan Library*

2002 *Earl Marischal*

Built	Doncaster
Into traffic	October 1934
Allocations	Doncaster, October 1934
	Haymarket, June 1935
	Dundee, June 1935
	Aberdeen Ferryhill, September 1936
Rebuilt as 'A2/2'	June 1944

Right:
No doubt organised by the LNER's Publicity Department, this stage-managed picture shows *Earl Marischal* alongside Gresley 'A1' Pacific No 2552 *Sansovino* and large-boilered Ivatt Atlantic No 3288.
Ian Allan Library

Below:
Earl Marischal received the streamlined casing during its first general overhaul in October 1936. Only 1,229 miles separate the total mileages of *Cock o' the North* and *Earl Marischal* as 'P2s', 360,907 being recorded by the latter.
Ian Allan Library

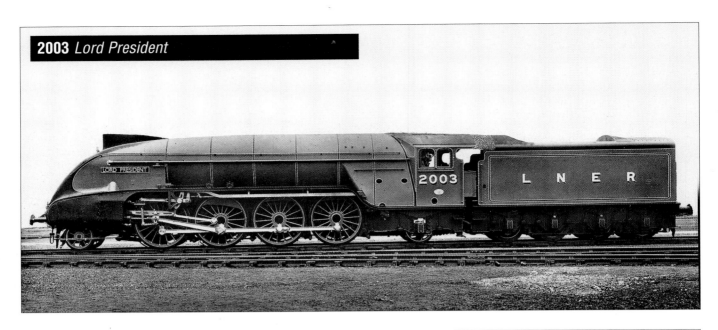

2003 *Lord President*

2003 *Lord President*

Built	Doncaster
Into traffic	June 1936
Allocations	Haymarket, June 1936
	Dundee, September 1936
	Haymarket, October 1942
Rebuilt as 'A2/2'	December 1944

Left:
An official photograph of No 2003 *Lord President*, with the 'A4' streamlining; note that the valance did not cover the driving wheels. These locomotives must have made an impressive sight in LNER apple green. No 2003 was observed at King's Cross only once prior to settling down to service in Scotland. *Ian Allan Library*

Below left:
Lord President lined up with what appears to be 'V2' 2-6-2 No 4771 *Green Arrow* outside the paint shop at Doncaster Works for an exhibition or open day on 20 June 1936.
Ian Allan Library

Above right:
Lord President being prepared for work on shed, probably Haymarket.
Ian Allan Library

Below:
Action shots of *Lord President* as a 'P2' appear to be difficult to find, but here we see the locomotive entering Kirkcaldy during 1936, heading the 9.0am from Aberdeen to Edinburgh. It is recorded as having covered 246,283 miles as a 'P2', giving it an annual mileage of around 29,000. *Ian Allan Library*

2004 *Mons Meg*

Built	Doncaster
Into traffic	July 1936
Allocations	Haymarket
Rebuilt as 'A2/2'	November 1944

Above:
Mons Meg entering Edinburgh Waverley with the morning express from Aberdeen on 11 July 1938. *J. B. Wilson / Rail Archive Stephenson*

Above right:
No 2004 *Mons Meg* was almost identical to No 2003 but was the only 'P2' to be fitted with a by-pass valve to divert part of the exhaust steam away from the blastpipe. It is seen when brand-new in 1936 at Grantham shed, ready to work a stopping train back to Doncaster. *T. G. Hepburn / Rail Archive Stephenson*

Right
A very fine picture of *Mons Meg* at Leuchars Junction with the 5.15pm express from Edinburgh to Aberdeen on 23 September 1938. The locomotive's total mileage as a 'P2' was 294,243 — an average of just over 36,000 miles per annum. *T. G. Hepburn / Rail Archive Stephenson*

2005 *Thane of Fife*	
Built	Doncaster
Into traffic	August 1936
Allocations	Dundee
Rebuilt as 'A2/2'	January 1943

Above:
No 2005 *Thane of Fife* leaves Aberdeen, heading an up express past Ferryhill shed, sometime in the late 1930s. *Ian Allan Library*

Below:
Thane of Fife at Eastfield shed early in 1939. This was the only member of the class to have a single chimney and blastpipe, which may be why it was the first to be selected for rebuilding as a Pacific. *C. Lawson-Kerr*

Above:
Another picture of *Thane of Fife*, believed to have been taken just south of Aberdeen. The locomotive spent its entire career as a 'P2' working fron Dundee shed.
F. R. Hebron / Rail Archive Stephenson

Below:
A portrait of *Thane of Fife* on the turntable at an unidentified shed. Being the first to be rebuilt, this locomotive covered a lower mileage than the other 'P2s', achieving just 225,739, but its annual average was similar to that of the others, at just under 35,000. *Ian Allan Library*

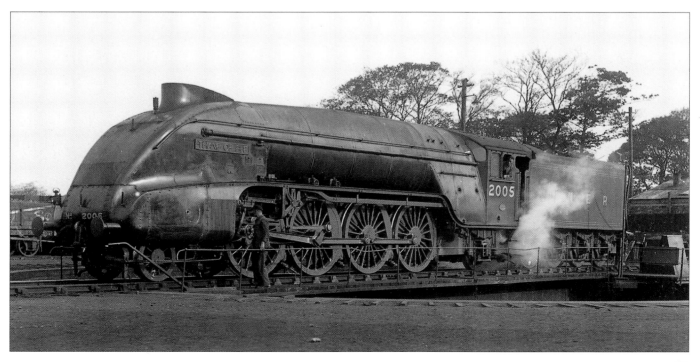

2006 Wolf of Badenoch

Built	Doncaster
Into traffic	September 1936
Allocations	Haymarket, September 1936
	Aberdeen Ferryhill, November 1936
	Haymarket, October 1942
Rebuilt as 'A2/2'	April 1944

Above
An official portrait of No 2006 *Wolf of Badenoch* taken upon completion of the locomotive in 1936.
Ian Allan Library

Below:
Wolf of Badenoch being serviced at Aberdeen Ferryhill shed in 1936. Along with the other Aberdeen-alloacted 'P2', No 2002 it was not allocated to regular crews, and divided its time between top-link passenger, fish and meat trains.
T. G. Hepburn / Rail Archive Stephenson

Above:
A side view of *Wolf of Badenoch* which emphasises the locomotive's powerful lines. It varied from the rest of the class in being fitted with a larger firebox and combustion chamber. *Ian Allan Library*

Below:
Wolf of Badenoch approaches Aberdeen with the 2.0pm Edinburgh–Aberdeen express on 19 August 1937. During the war years the class was painted unlined black and the fairing ahead of the cylinder covers was removed. No 2006 is credited with a total of 287,187 miles, giving it an annual mileage average of around 37,000. *E. R. Wethersett*

Above:
The six 'P2' 2-8-2s designed by Gresley for the difficult Edinburgh–Aberdeen route proved unsatisfactory, the wheelbase being unsuitable for the route's almost continuous curves. Thompson's solution was to rebuild them as Pacifics, as the 'A2/2' class. In 1949 all were transferred south to England, where they would remain until withdrawn. By now renumbered 60501, *Cock o' the North* awaits its next duty at Grantham shed on 23 August 1952. *J. P. Wilson / Rail Archive Stephenson*

Left:
Cock o' the North in charge of the up 'Queen of Scots' Pullman in the mid-1950s. Passing Northallerton signalbox, the train is slowing to take the now lifted line to Harrogate via Ripon. The 'A2/2' would work as far as Leeds Central, where the train reversed. *J. W. Hague / N. Stead collection*

60501 *Cock o' the North*

Rebuilt	Doncaster
Into traffic	14 September 1944
Renumbered	501, 11 August 1946
	60501, 22 May 1948
Allocations	Haymarket, 14 September 1944
	Aberdeen Ferryhill, 29 October 1944
	Haymarket, 4 September 1949
	York, 27 November 1949
	Neville Hill, Leeds, 27 November 1950
	York, 17 December 1950
Withdrawn	8 February 1960; scrapped at
	Doncaster Works

Right:
The 'A2/2s' were not frequent visitors to Nottingham Victoria, but on 20 April 1954 *Cock o' the North* (still retaining the original straight-sided chimney) was present, having worked an empty-stock train from as far south as Banbury. *T. G. Hepburn / Rail Archive Stephenson*

Right:
One month before its final general repair, *Cock o' the North* passes Fulwell, Sunderland, with a King's Cross–Newcastle express on 1 August 1958. *D. M. C. Hepburne-Scott / Rail Archive Stephenson*

Left:
Six weeks after being condemned, *Cock o' the North* stands at the back of Doncaster Works in March 1960 with assorted ex-Midland locomotives for scrap. It had covered 616,461 miles in its 15½ years as an 'A2/2', giving a low annual mileage average of under 40,000. Amazingly it still had its nameplates attached — how times have changed! *Gavin Morrison*

As rebuilt all six 'A2/2s' were turned out in wartime black, but in March 1947 Cowlairs Works repainted *Earl Marischal* in LNER apple green with Gill Sans lettering. No details are available for this picture, but judging by the locomotive's clean state it could well have been taken at the works. *P. Ransome-Wallis*

60502 *Earl Marischal*	
Rebuilt	Doncaster
Into traffic	23 June 1944
Renumbered	502, 12 May 1946
	60502, 30 June 1948
Allocations	Aberdeen Ferryhill, 23 June 1944
	Haymarket, 4 September 1949
	York, 27 November 1949
Withdrawn	3 July 1961; scrapped at
	Doncaster Works

Above:
Earl Marischal had only recently been transferred to York when this picture was taken on 8 August 1950. Working a down goods on the East Coast main line at Croft Spa, it retains apple-green livery with 'L N E R' on the tender, but with BR numbers. *W. Rogerson / Rail Archive Stephenson*

Left:
Now in BR Brunswick green, which it would have received during general repair in March 1951, *Earl Marischal* heads a York–King's Cross express past Potters Bar on 12 May 1951. *Brian Morrison*

Above:
Two 'A2/2s' side by side at Grantham shed on 5 September 1953. Both are York locomotives and in terrible condition externally. *Lord President* (left) has the 'Northumbrian' headboard in place. *Earl Marischal* was the only 'P2'/'A2/2' to cover over one million miles in service — 360,907 as a 'P2' and 673,947 as an 'A2/2' — averaging 38,686 per annum.
T. G. Hepburn /
Rail Archive Stephenson

Right:
Now with cast-iron chimney and in clean condition, *Earl Marischal* passes York shed as it heads north on a cross-country working to Newcastle, probably *c*1955. *Eric Treacy*

Right:
Top-link work for *Earl Marischal* as it heads past Naburn with the up 'Norseman', the boat train from Newcastle to King's Cross. No date is available, but the photograph was probably taken in the early 1950s.
C. Ord

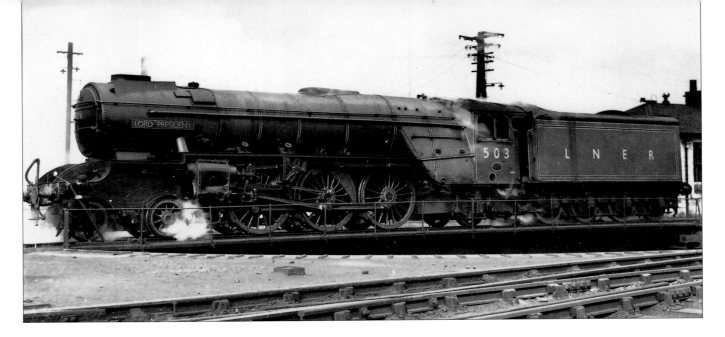

60503 *Lord President*

Rebuilt	Doncaster
Into traffic	17 December 1944
Renumbered	503, 30 June 1946
	60503, 18 September 1948
Allocations	King's Cross, 17 December 1944
	Gateshead, 2 February 1945
	Haymarket, 20 March 1945
	King's Cross, 11 April 1945
	Haymarket, 13 May 1945
	Aberdeen Ferryhill, 17 May 1948
	Haymarket, 26 May 1948
	York, 27 November 1949
	Neville Hill, Leeds, 27 November 1950
	York, 17 December 1950
Withdrawn	27 November 1959; scrapped at Doncaster Works

Above:
In December 1946 *Lord President* was repainted by Cowlairs Works in apple-green livery with Gill Sans-style lettering, as seen here at Haymarket shed in Edinburgh. *N. Stead collection*

Below:
This fine undated picture of *Lord President* shows the locomotive passing through Marsh Lane Cutting, east of Leeds, with a Newcastle–Liverpool express. This could have been during the period in 1950 when Nos 60501 and 60503 were allocated to Neville Hill shed, when some of its 'A3s' were out of action. *K. Field / Rail Archive Stephenson*

Right:
Four months before a general repair, *Lord President* heads an up express up Gamston Bank on 14 April 1956. Around this time York shed's passenger diagrams were often 'A2/2'-hauled, although only one of these ran in daylight. *D. Marriott*

Above:
Lord President and *Thane of Fife* were the first 'A2/2s' to be withdrawn, in November 1959. The former is seen heading an up express past Great Porton and towards Stoke Tunnel on 4 August 1959. As an 'A2/2' it covered just 246,238 miles, which works out at a very low annual average of less than 18,000. *T. G. Hepburn / Rail Archive Stephenson*

60504 *Mons Meg*

Rebuilt	Doncaster
Into traffic	3 November 1944
Renumbered	504, 30 June 1946
	e504, 12 March 1948
	60504, 23 March 1948
Allocations	Haymarket, 3 November 1944
	New England, 9 January 1950
Withdrawn	23 January 1961; scrapped at
	Doncaster Works

Above:
Regular duties for the New England 'A2/2s' in the early 1950s were the Peterborough–King's Cross semi-fasts, No 60504 *Mons Meg* being seen thus employed near Potters Bar on 12 May 1951. *Brian Morrison*

Right:
Mons Meg reaches journey's end as it enters King's Cross with an up express *c*1958. *M. Welch*

Above:
Having been released from its train, *Mons Meg* pauses at the end of the platform at King's Cross before backing out to 'Top Shed' for servicing. *Mons Meg* recorded the highest mileage of the 'A2/2s' at New England, at 294,242, which given its later withdrawal date only just betters *Lord President*'s average of around 18,000 per annum. *M. Welch*

Right:
Working an up semi-fast from Peterborough to King's Cross, *Mons Meg* passes Hatfield on 28 February 1959. *I. S. Carr*

Left:
The first 'P2' to be rebuilt as a Pacific was No 2005 *Thane of Fife*, so treated over the winter of 1942/3. In April 1946 it was renumbered 994 but ran thus for less than three weeks, making this a rare photograph. The locomotive is seen at Haymarket shed on 1 May 1946, during its 6½ years there as a Pacific. *Rail Archive Stephenson*

Centre left:
After rebuilding *Thane of Fife* ran nameless for 18 months. By now numbered 505, it is seen in wartime unlined black livery with abbreviated 'N E' on the tender on 22 June 1946 at Doncaster Works, where it was awaiting a general overhaul. It would emerge still in black but with the full 'L N E R' restored, finally regaining apple green in January 1948, albeit with 'BRITISH RAILWAYS' on the tender. *T. G. Hepburn / Rail Archive Stephenson*

Below:
Having adopted its BR identity as No 60505, *Thane of Fife* leaves York on 10 April 1956 at the head of the 8.35am Glasgow Queen Street–King's Cross, which it would have taken over at Newcastle. *Gavin Morrison*

60505 *Thane of Fife*

Rebuilt	Doncaster
Into traffic	18 January 1943
Renumbered	994, 25 April 1946
	505, 12 May 1946
	60505, 5 June 1948
Allocations	Doncaster, 18 January 1943
	Haymarket, 3 April 1943
	New England, 30 December 1949
Withdrawn	10 November 1959; scrapped at
	Doncaster Works

Above:
In December 1949 *Thane of Fife* moved south from Scotland to (New) England, where it would remain for the rest of its career. It is seen with an up express at Gainsbrough in May 1956. *D. Penney*

Below:
Thane of Fife at Doncaster Works for an unclassified repair on 19 April 1959. Note that, even by this late date, it had still not received a cast-iron chimney, meaning that it can have run so fitted for a maximum of just seven months. This locomotive, which would receive its final general repair in September 1959, would achieve the lowest mileage of any 'A2/2' — 225,739, giving an incredibly low annual average of under 14,000. *Gavin Morrison*

60506 *Wolf of Badenoch*

Rebuilt	Doncaster
Into traffic	15 April 1944
Renumbered	506, 30 June 1946
	60506, 18 December 1948
Allocations	Haymarket, 15 April 1944
	Aberdeen Ferryhill, 8 April 1949
	Haymarket, 15 May 1949
	New England, 20 November 1949
Withdrawn	4 April 1961; scrapped at
	Doncaster Works

Above:
In apple green but renumbered 60506 and with
'BRITISH RAILWAYS' on the tender. *Wolf of Badenoch* passes
Inverkeithing with the 2.15pm Edinburgh
Waverley–Aberdeen on 6 August 1949. Allocated to
Haymarket, it would work this train as far as Dundee.
No 60506 would run in apple green for only around a year,
before receiving Brunswick green in July 1950.
E. R. Wethersett

Below:
Having moved south to New England in November 1949,
Wolf of Badenoch is pictured on Gamston Bank at the head
of an up express in 1956. *D. Penney*

Right:
Wolf of Badenoch was the last of the New England 'A2/2s' to survive. Given its average annual mileage of just under 17,000, it must have spent a lot of time inside New England with a 'not to be moved' sign on its tender, as seen here on 24 May 1959.
Brian Morrison

Centre right:
This time in steam under the coaler at New England, *Wolf of Badenoch* is prepared for its next duty. The date is recorded as 22 May 1948, but this is clearly incorrect, as the locomotive retained its LNER number until December of that year and received Brunswick green only in July 1950.
J. F. Davies / Rail Archive Stephenson

Below right:
Wolf of Badenoch was the only 'A2/2' never to run with a cast-iron chimney. Having received its final general repair seven months earlier, it is seen awaiting its next duty at King's Cross 'Top Shed' on 14 September 1958. The 'A2/2s' were never popular with crews or considered a success, always being overshadowed by the many other East Coast Pacifics. There seem to be few recorded interesting performances, but this is hardly surprising, given their low mileages.
Gavin Morrison

60507 *Highland Chieftain*

Built	Darlington
Into traffic	13 May 1944 as No 3696
Renumbered	507, 12 May 1946
	60507, 29 October 1948
Allocations	Darlington, 13 May 1944
	Heaton, 8 June 1944
	King's Cross, 16 November 1944
	Haymarket, 15 December 1949
	St Margarets, 13 July 1960
Withdrawn	12 December 1960; scrapped at Doncaster Works

Left:
The four 'A2/1s' were begun as 'V2s', and the type was effectively a Pacific conversion of the 'V2'. The first locomotive, No 3696, was renumbered 507 on 12 May 1946 and is seen at Greenwood with a down express in 1947, by now running with the tender from 'A4' No 4469 *Sir Ralph Wedgwood*, withdrawn as a result of damage sustained in a bombing raid at York shed in 1942. *Rail Archive Stephenson*

Below left:
In May 1947 No 507 was named *Highland Chieftain*. In a scene unlikely to please clean-air enthusiasts the locomotive makes a dramatic departure from King's Cross on 28 April 1948. The 'A2/1s' were shared equally between Eastern and Scottish Regions until 15 December 1949, when *Highland Chieftain* moved to Haymarket, thereby becoming the only example of all the 'A2' variants to be allocated to Eastern, North Eastern and Scottish Regions. *C. C. B. Herbert*

Above right:
In its 10 years allocated to Haymarket *Highland Chieftain* was used on all the main-line diagrams except the non-stoppers to King's Cross. Here, with the help of a banker, it is climbing the 1-in-41 Cowlairs Bank with a late-afternoon express from Glasgow Queen Street to Edinburgh Waverley in April 1955. *Gavin Morrison*

Centre right:
Highland Chieftain bursts out of the Mound Tunnel in Edinburgh's Princes Street Gardens at the head of the 2.15pm express to Aberdeen on 22 June 1954. The locomotive had received BR Brunswick green in October 1949. *E. D. Bruton*

Below right:
Highland Chieftain heads a Perth–Edinburgh Waverley express past Milepost 26 near Blairadman in the late 1950s. This locomotive would cover a total of 786,505 miles in its career. *W. J. V. Anderson / Rail Archive Stephenson*

60508 *Duke of Rothesay*

Built	Darlington
Into traffic	30 June 1944 as No 3697
Renumbered	508, 20 July 1946
	E508, 6 February 1948
	60508, 26 May 1948
Allocations	Darlington, 30 June 1944
	King's Cross, 25 November 1944
	Gorton, 10 February 1945
	King's Cross, 28 February 1945
	New England, 4 June 1950
Withdrawn	20 February 1961; scrapped at Doncaster Works

Above:
Duke of Rothesay was the only 'A2/1' to spend its entire career in the Eastern Region, and as such it seems to have been photographed much more than were its Scottish sisters. This picture was taken outside Darlington paint shop in January 1947. *Ian Allan Library*

Below:
Duke of Rothesay heads an up express near Potters Bar *c*1947, while allocated to King's Cross. *R. F. Dearden*

Right:
With 'KING'S +' on the buffer-beam and 'L N E R' on the 'V2'-type tender, *Duke of Rothesay* makes a fine sight as it emerges from Welwyn North Tunnel with a King's Cross–Peterborough slow train in 1947. This locomotive had been allocated to Gorton shed for two weeks in early 1945. *F. R. Hebron / Rail Archive Stephenson*

Right:
Duke of Rothesay was the only 'A2/1' to run with the 'E' prefix to its LNER number. Following a light repair in May 1948 this was changed to 60508, but 'L N E R' was retained on the tender. This picture shows the locomotive passing Grantham with a Leeds Central–King's Cross express on 17 June 1948. *J. P. Wilson / Rail Archive Stephenson*

Left:
Duke of Rothesay was involved in a serious accident at New Southgate on 17 July 1948, when it overturned at around 70mph at the head of the 7.50pm Edinburgh–King's Cross. The accident, in which the fireman was killed, was blamed on a track fault in Barnet Tunnel. The locomotive took two months to repair at Doncaster Works. *F. R. Hebron / Rail Archive Stephenson*

Right:
Now allocated to New England, *Duke of Rothesay*, in fine condition, prepares to leave King's Cross with the 10.5pm 'Junior Scotsman' on 23 May 1952. *C. R. L. Coles / Rail Archive Stephenson*

Left:
The fireman looks relaxed as *Duke of Rothesay* makes an impressive departure from King's Cross with the 'Junior Scotsman' on 23 May 1952. *C. R. L. Coles / Rail Archive Stephenson*

Centre right:
With a badly burned smokebox door and in generally poor condition externally, *Duke of Rothesay* climbs past Eaton Crossing, south of Retford, with an up express in 1956. *D. Penney*

Below:
It would appear that *Duke of Rothesay* received its cast-iron chimney during a general repair at Doncaster in February 1957, being shown thus fitted passing Essendine with a King's Cross–Newcastle express on 3 August 1957. Given that it was so frequently photographed, it is surprising to note that this locomotive achieved the lowest mileage (754,952) of the sub-class. *P. H. Wells*

60509 *Waverley*

Built	Darlington
Into traffic	15 November 1944 as No 3698
Renumbered	509, 2 May 1946
	60509, 6 August 1948
Allocations	Darlington, 15 November 1944
	Haymarket, 14 March 1945
	Aberdeen Ferryhill, 4 September 1949
	Haymarket, 25 September 1949
Withdrawn	15 August 1960; scrapped at
	Doncaster Works

Above:
New as Nos 3696-9, the 'A2/1s' were renumbered as 507-10 in 1946 and again as 60507-10 following nationalisation. All had been named by April 1948. Here we see No 60509 *Waverley*, by now in apple green with 'BRITISH RAILWAYS' on the tender, ready to leave Aberdeen with an up express on 28 August 1949. For some reason the numbers were placed slightly lower than on the other members of the sub-class. The large smoke-deflectors had been fitted in October 1946. *J. P. Wilson / Rail Archive Stephenson*

Above right:
With the North British Hotel dominating the Edinburgh skyline, *Waverley* prepares to leave 'its' station on 20 February 1954 with a local service. This had been the last of the sub-class to receive Brunswick green, in June 1950. *G. M. Staddon / N. Stead collection*

Right:
With only six months left in active service, *Waverley* coasts down the gradient off the Tay Bridge towards Dundee during February 1960. This locomotive achieved the highest mileage of the four 'A2/1s', its total of 818,943 giving an annual average of around 51,000. *A. Coupar*

60510 *Robert the Bruce*

Right:
Its 64B shedplate proclaiming allocation to Haymarket, a spotless *Robert the Bruce* stands outside St Margarets shed in the mid-1950s. Around this time Haymarket's Pacifics were kept immaculate, and it is very difficult to tell from the picture whether or not No 60510 was ex works. *N. Stead collection*

Below right:
The fireman appears to have things well under control as *Robert the Bruce* storms Cockburnspath Bank with the up 'Heart of Midlothian' on 11 September 1954. This locomotive would cover 815,528 miles in service — just 3,500 less than *Waverley*, giving a similar annual average of around 51,000. *W. J. V. Anderson / Rail Archive Stephenson*

Above:
A very early picture of No 3699 in plain black and yet to be named *Robert the Bruce*, taken at Waverley station (looking east) during December 1945. The smoke-deflectors were not added until April 1948. Until March 1949 the sub-class was maintained by Darlington Works. *C. R. L. Coles / Rail Archive Stephenson*

Below:
While allocated to Haymarket the 'A2/1s' were used regularly on passenger trains over the Waverley route. By now renumbered 60510, *Robert the Bruce* enters Melrose with an up express in the mid-1950s. *N. Stead collection*

60510 *Robert the Bruce*

Built	Darlington
Into traffic	13 January 1945 as No 3699
Renumbered	510, 7 June 1946
	60510, 28 April 1948
Allocations	Darlington, 13 January 1945
	Haymarket, 1 March 1945
	Aberdeen Ferryhill, 4 September 1949
	Haymarket, 25 September 1949
	St Margarets, 13 July 1960
Withdrawn	21 November 1960; scrapped at Doncaster Works

60500 *Edward Thompson*

Built	Doncaster
Into traffic	24 May 1946 as No 500
Renumbered	e500, 26 February 1948
	60500, 7 October 1949
Allocations	Gateshead, 24 May 1946
	King's Cross, 7 June 1946
	Doncaster, 20 July 1946
	King's Cross, 12 September 1946
	New England, 4 June 1950
Withdrawn	16 June 1963; to Doncaster Works for
	scrap, 2 September 1963

Above:

A fine portrait of No 500 *Edward Thompson* as it entered service, seen at Doncaster shed on 1 September 1946, when only three months old. It attracted much attention for various reasons, being the first Pacific built at Doncaster for almost eight years and the 2,000th locomotive to be built at 'The Plant'. The LNER Board decided it should be named after the outgoing CME, the naming ceremony taking place at Marylebone station. The design incorporated many new features, and the locomotive was initially used on easy duties based at Gateshead. In fact it ran hot at Retford on its first outing, causing some embarrassment. Trials were conducted against a 'V2' but seemed to be dogged by bad luck or poor preparation, as poor-quality coal caused trouble and the driver did not rise to the occasion, being totally unfamiliar with the locomotive. Eventually it was transferred south to King's Cross, where it was used on top-link work, as the older 'A3' and 'A4' Pacifics were in poor shape after the war years. It soon became clear that the locomotive was very powerful and more than capable of carrying out its duties on the East Coast main line. As can be seen, it received full apple green livery and full shaded lettering and numbers. *E. R. Wethersett*

Above:
There are no details about this photograph, but it appears to have been taken just outside York and depicts No 500 with a down train, which would have been the 1.50pm Leeds–Newcastle, between 5 and 7 November 1946, when the test runs were carried out. *C. C. B. Herbert*

Below:
At the end of the long climb up Stoke Bank, *Edward Thompson* (by now numbered 60500) passes the signalbox at the summit with a King's Cross–Newcastle express on 30 July 1951. *E. R. Wethersett*

Left:
A fine but regrettably undated picture of *Edward Thompson* approaching Holbeck High Level station at Leeds, which would close to passengers on 7 July 1958. The photograph must have been taken prior to July 1958, as from that month the code for New England shed (where the locomotive was then allocated) was changed from 35A to 34E. *J. P. Wilson / Rail Archive Stephenson*

Below left:
Edward Thompson heads south near Markham Moor with an up express on a hot summer's day in 1958. *D. Penney*

Right:
The down 'Heart of Midlothian' was for many years a regular New England 'A2' working as far as Newcastle. On 4 August 1959 *Edward Thompson* descends from Stoke Summit past Great Porton station, closed to passengers since 15 September 1958. *T. G. Hepburn / Rail Archive Stephenson*

Below:
Edward Thompson was late in having its cast-iron chimney fitted, probably during its general overhaul in March 1960. The locomotive is seen arriving at Newcastle with an express from King's Cross on 16 July 1960. *R. Leslie*

60511 *Airborne*

Built	Doncaster
Into traffic	20 July 1946 as No 511
Renumbered	60511, 16 April 1948
Allocations	Gateshead, 20 July 1946
	Heaton, 8 September 1946
	Tweedmouth, 1 October 1961
Withdrawn	12 November 1962; to Doncaster
	Works for scrap, 30 April 1963

Left:
Airborne at Grantham shed on 6 October 1947. The large unshaded number (511) is clearly visible, but the 'L N E R' lettering on the tender is obscured by grime.
T. G. Hepburn / Rail Archive Stephenson

Left:
Now with front numberplate displaying its BR number (60511) and with 'BRITISH RAILWAYS' on the tender, *Airborne* passes Prestonpans with an up goods on 23 April 1948, a week after it emerged from its first general overhaul at Doncaster. *E. R. Wethersett*

Left:
Double-headed Pacifics on the ECML were fairly rare. Here *Airborne* pilots 'A1' No 60126 *Sir Vincent Raven* into Durham station on a Bristol–Newcastle express in the early 1950s.
Ian Allan Library

Above:
Airborne leaves York on 6 July 1957 at the head of the 8.5 Birmingham New Street–Newcastle, having taken over from a Stanier Class 5 4-6-0.
M. Mensing

Right:
Airborne ready to leave Newcastle with the 3.30pm to Birmingham New Street on 9 April 1960.
I. S. Carr

Below:
Airborne stands dead in York shed yard on 5 June 1960. *Gavin Morrison*

Above:
No 60512 *Steady Aim* on Grantham shed, looking very smart in apple green, with larger (12in) cabside numerals and 'BRITISH RAILWAYS' on the tender. This locomotive and No 60514 were the only two to have the BR number painted on the buffer-beam. *J. P. Wilson / Rail Archive Stephenson*

Left:
Looking well cleaned by Heaton shed, *Steady Aim* passes Peterborough North 'box as it approaches the station platform with an up express on Sunday 22 April 1951. *P. H. Wells*

60512 *Steady Aim*

Built	Doncaster
Into traffic	24 August 1946 as No 512
Renumbered	60512, 20 March 1948
Allocations	Gateshead, 24 August 1946
	Heaton, 8 September 1946
	York, 14 December 1952
	St Margarets, 2 December 1962
	Polmadie, 15 September 1963
	Dundee, 14 June 1965
Withdrawn	19 June 1965; sold to Motherwell Machinery & Scrap Co, July 1965

Left:
Top-link work for *Steady Aim* as it heads away from Newcastle into the evening sunshine with the up 'Talisman' on the afternoon of 21 April 1960. *I. S. Carr*

Above:
Diverted because of engineering work between Hitchin and Peterborough, *Steady Aim* passes Trumpington Yard, Cambridge, with the 4.35pm King's Cross–York express on 29 May 1960, by which time the locomotive was allocated to York shed. *G. D. King*

Below:
Steady Aim at Doncaster Works for its last visit — an unclassified repair — on 3 March 1963. By now a St Margarets engine, it was very clean for one of that shed's stud and would put in another 27 months' service in Scotland before withdrawal. *Gavin Morrison*

60513 *Dante*

Above:
Nos 513-9 emerged new from Doncaster with shaded numbers and lettering. Pictured when only a week old, No 513 *Dante* passes Ardsley with the 12.50pm local stopping train from Leeds Central to Doncaster, which was being used as a running-in turn. Ardsley station would close to passengers from 6 November 1964. *A. E. Woodhouse*

Right:
After its second general overhaul *Dante* received its BR number (60513) and 'BRITISH RAILWAYS' on the tender. This very powerful picture shows the locomotive passing Potters Bar with the 4pm King's Cross–Leeds Central in 1949. *F. R. Hebron / Rail Archive Stephenson*

Left:
In immaculate external condition, which was unusual for New England locomotives, *Dante* passes Potters Bar with an express from Edinburgh Waverley to King's Cross on 12 May 1951. *Brian Morrison*

60513 *Dante*	
Built	Doncaster
Into traffic	31 August 1946 as No 513
Renumbered	60513, 3 November 1948
Allocations	King's Cross, 31 August 1946
	New England, 19 December 1948
	Grantham, 8 June 1958
	New England, 14 June 1959
Withdrawn	27 April 1963; to Doncaster Works for scrap, 1 May 1963

Above:
In charge of the down 'Heart of Midlothian', a regular duty for New England 'A2s', *Dante* puts up a good exhaust as it passes Stevenage on 1 August 1955. Note that the train's headboard has been affixed the wrong way around! *E. R. Wethersett*

Right:
Another picture of *Dante* heading the down 'Heart of Midlothian', this time passing Pilmoor, 16 miles north of York, on 18 June 1961, looking less than clean two months ahead of its last general repair. *Gavin Morrison*

60514 *Chamossaire*

Built	Doncaster
Into traffic	28 September 1946 as No 514
Renumbered	60514, 23 March 1948
Allocations	King's Cross, 28 September 1946
	New England, 19 December 1948
Withdrawn	29 December 1962; to Doncaster
	Works for scrap, 4 June 1963

Above:

Chamossaire would turn out to be the most camera-shy of all the 'A2/3s'. It was also unique amongst the 'A2/3s' in that it never received a cast-iron chimney. Following an initial spell working from King's Cross it put in 14 years' service at New England and is pictured climbing Holloway Bank with the down 'Aberdonian' on 11 May 1954. *Brian Morrison*

Above right:

Without a trace of exhaust *Chamossaire* climbs the bank at Markham Moor with an up express in 1957. *D. Penney*

Right:

With just seven months to go before being withdrawal, *Chamossaire* passes Newcastle on the goods line with an up tank train on 21 May 1962. *M. Mensing*

60515 *Sun Stream*

Built	Doncaster
Into traffic	19 October 1946 as No 515
Renumbered	60515, 25 June 1948
Allocations	Heaton, 19 October 1946
	Gateshead, 6 July 1952
	York, 14 December 1952
Withdrawn	12 November 1962; to Doncaster
	Works for scrap, 9 April 1963

Left:
An evocative backlit shot of No 60515 *Sun Stream* at the head of a Newcastle–King's Cross express leaving Grantham on 11 February 1950. *J. Cupit*

Above:
A study of *Sun Stream* at rest at an unidentified shed — possibly its then home of York — in the mid-1950s. *P. Ransome-Wallis*

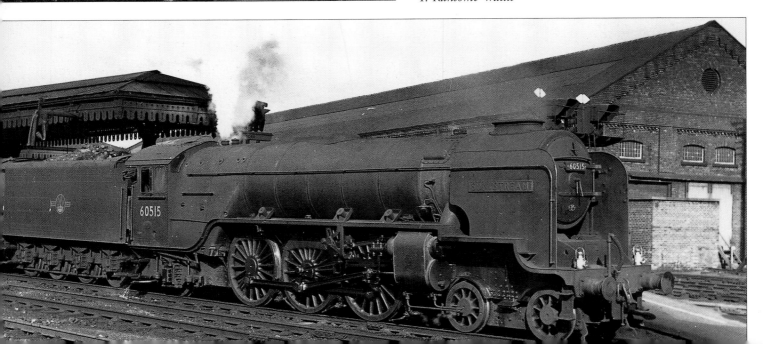

Below left:
In 1956 *Sun Stream* received the later BR emblem on its tender, as seen in this picture taken at York on 13 July 1959. Note that the locomotive also now has a lipped chimney. *J. C. Haydon*

Right:
Crossing the bridge over the River Wear, *Sun Stream* approaches Sunderland station with the 12.5pm from Newcastle to Colchester on 23 March 1961. The 'A2/3' would work as far as York, where a March 'V2' was booked to take over. *D. J. Dippie*

Below:
With coal piled high in the tender, *Sun Stream* awaits its next duty at York shed on 6 August 1961. By the time it was withdrawn in November 1962 it had accumulated just 690,352 miles. *Gavin Morrison*

60516 Hycilla

Built	Doncaster
Into traffic	2 November 1946 as No 516
Renumbered	60516, 8 October 1948
Allocations	Heaton, 2 November 1946
	Gateshead, 6 July 1952
	Heaton, 22 May 1960
	York, 12 June 1960
Withdrawn	12 November 1962; to Doncaster Works
	for scrap, 1 April 1963

Left:
An admiring crowd has gathered around *Hycilla* as it prepares to leave King's Cross with a down express. The 52B (Heaton) shedplate just discernible on the smokebox suggests the photograph was taken prior to July 1952, when the locomotive was transferred to Gateshead.
Ian Allan Library

Below left:
Climbing Gamston Bank, with gradients varying between 1 in 178 and 1 in 200, *Hycilla* heads for King's Cross with an up express on 5 August 1958.
D. Marriott

Above right:
Hycilla approaches Sandy at the head of the 12.20pm Hull–King's Cross on August Bank Holiday (7 August) 1961. *M. Mensing*

Below:
With the Minster visible above the dome, *Hycilla* stands dead in York shed yard on 12 March 1962. By this time there was little work for York's Pacifics, and *Hycilla* would be withdrawn in November, having covered 833,050 miles in 16 years of service, thereby averaging 1,000 miles per week. *Gavin Morrison*

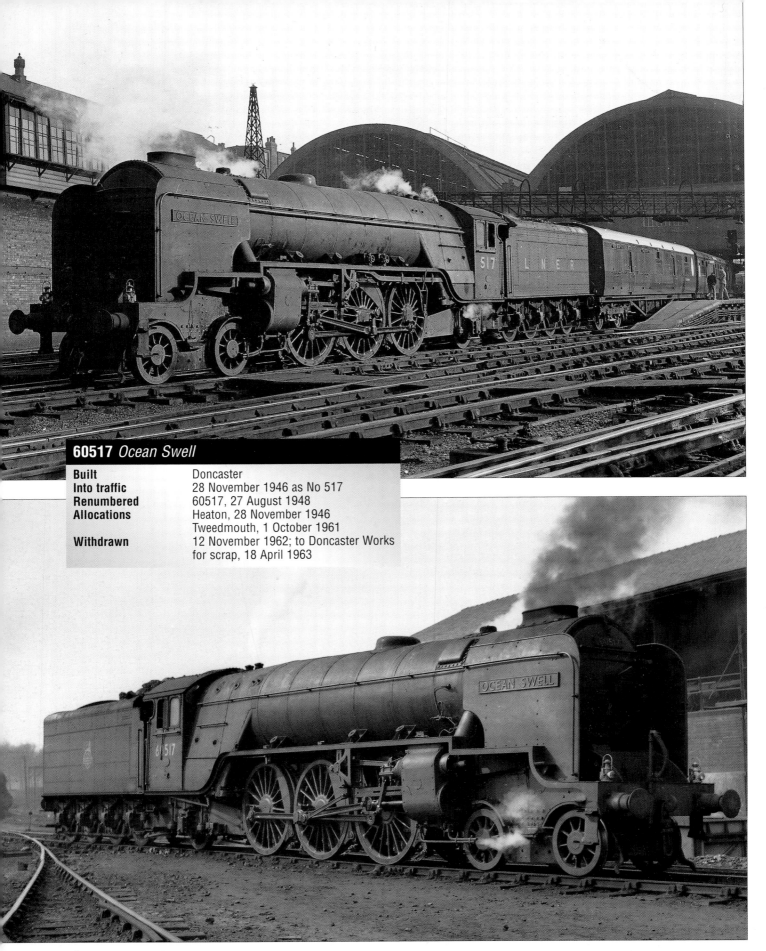

60517 *Ocean Swell*

Built	Doncaster
Into traffic	28 November 1946 as No 517
Renumbered	60517, 27 August 1948
Allocations	Heaton, 28 November 1946
	Tweedmouth, 1 October 1961
Withdrawn	12 November 1962; to Doncaster Works
	for scrap, 18 April 1963

Left:
Displaying the shaded numbers and letters it received when new, No 517 *Ocean Swell* stands at King's Cross Platform 10 prior to leaving with the 5.30pm to Newcastle on 22 March 1948. *C. C. B. Herbert / Rail Archive Stephenson*

Below left:
Although 'A1s', 'A2s' and 'A4s' were regular visitors to Leeds Neville Hill shed, photographs seem quite rare. *Ocean Swell* is seen by the coaling stage in the early 1950s. *D. Penney*

Above right:
In fine condition externally *Ocean Swell* heads south past Newark with an up express in April 1956. The lines on the left were part of the now closed route to/from Nottingham via Carlton. *D. Penney*

Below:
After 15 years at Heaton *Ocean Swell* spent its last year of service at Tweedmouth. Minus shedplate, it is seen at Berwick-upon-Tweed station, having worked the 3.30pm local from Edinburgh, on 24 May 1962. *M. Mensing*

60518 *Tehran*

Built	Doncaster
Into traffic	28 December 1946 as No 518
Renumbered	60518, 15 July 1948
Allocations	Gateshead, 28 December 1946
	Heaton, 25 February 1960
	York, 12 June 1960
Withdrawn	12 November 1962; to Doncaster Works
	for scrap, 28 March 1963

Above left:
Only seven months old, No 518 *Tehran* passes Morpeth with the 1.4pm Newcastle–Edinburgh Waverley during July 1947. *J. Watson*

Below left:
The following month *Tehran* leaves Newcastle with a down express. The shading of the numbers and lettering shows up particularly well in this picture. *E. R. Wethersett*

Above:
During its first general overhaul, in July 1948, *Tehran* received its BR number (60518) and 'BRITISH RAILWAYS' lettering on the tender. Here in 1949 it is passing through Edinburgh's Princes Street Gardens on its way to Waverley station, where it will take out an up express.
W. J. V. Anderson /
Rail Archive Stephenson

Centre right:
Having worked south from Newcastle on a Liverpool train or even the up 'Queen of Scots', *Tehran* is coaled at Leeds Neville Hill shed ready for the return working. *D. Penney*

Right:
Hemmed in by other locomotives in York shed yard, *Tehran* awaits its next duty on 25 June 1960. This locomotive covered 825,230 miles in service.
Gavin Morrison

60519 *Honeyway*

Built	Doncaster
Into traffic	1 February 1947 as No 519
Renumbered	60519, 22 October 1948
Allocations	Haymarket, 1 February 1947
	St Margarets, 16 October 1961
	York, 2 December 1962
	('paper' transfer only)
Withdrawn	18 December 1962; to Doncaster Works
	for scrap

Left:
No 519 *Honeyway* was the only 'A2/3' to be allocated new to Scotland and would spend its entire career at Haymarket shed, save for a final 14 months at St Margarets. Sometime shortly after October 1948, when it received its BR number, the locomotive is seen backing through Edinburgh's Princes Street Gardens prior to working an express to Glasgow Queen Street or the north. *W. J. V. Anderson / Rail Archive Stephenson*

Below left:
Scottish 'A2s' of all types were regular performers on express freight as well as on top-link passenger duties. Here *Honeyway* crosses the Forth Bridge with an up fish or meat train on 10 August 1949. *E. R. Wethersett*

Above right:
With headboard reversed, *Honeyway* blows off steam as it climbs the 1-in-90 from Berwick-upon-Tweed to Burnmouth with a down express on 11 August 1954. *W. J. V. Anderson / Rail Archive Stephenson*

Centre right:
Top-link work for *Honeyway* as it passes the many sidings around Craigentinny near the end of its journey on the down 'Talisman' *c*1961. *W. J. V. Anderson / Rail Archive Stephenson*

Right:
Honeyway was seldom seen south of Newcastle other than when *en route* to or from Doncaster Works. Here it is passing Otterington, three miles south of Northallerton on a down special on 23 May 1961. One month later it entered Doncaster for its last general repair, when (presumably) it would receive its cast-iron chimney, as records state that No 60514 was the only member of the sub-class to retain the old-style version. *R. Leslie*

Left:
No 520 *Owen Tudor* was the first of the last five 'A2/3s' (Nos 520-4) to revert to Gill Sans characters on the apple-green livery. These can be seen in this picture of the locomotive preparing to leave King's Cross on a down express in 1947. *C. Turner / Rail Archive Stephenson*

60520 *Owen Tudor*

Built	Doncaster
Into traffic	29 March 1947 as No 520
Renumbered	60520, 22 October 1948
Allocations	Doncaster, 29 March 1947
	New England, 12 December 1948
	Grantham, 15 September 1952
	New England, 14 June 1959
	Doncaster, 10 January 1960
	New England, 23 September 1962
Withdrawn	16 June 1963; to Doncaster Works for scrap, 29 August 1963

Left:
Now with British Railways numbering (60520) and lettering, *Owen Tudor* heads a down express near Stevenage *c*1950. *R. F. Dearden*

Left:
A fine picture of *Owen Tudor*, now in Brunswick green, bursting out of Hadley Wood Tunnel with an express for York in June 1954. *Geoff Rixon*

Right:
Owen Tudor heads an up parcels train near Oakleigh Park in the late 1950s or early 1960s. The proximity of the track workers to the down main line would cause consternation to today's Health & Safety Executive!
Derek Cross

Above:
During its spell at Doncaster shed in the early 1960s *Owen Tudor* frequently worked the Leeds Central–Doncaster stopping trains. Here it is approaching Beeston, on the outskirts of Leeds, with the 2.5pm from Leeds Central on 28 August 1961. *Gavin Morrison*

Right:
Another view of *Owen Tudor* on a Leeds Central–Doncaster stopper, this time passing Copley Hill shed (56C) on 6 July 1961. *Gavin Morrison*

60521 *Watling Street*

Left:
A powerful picture of No 521 *Watling Street* in LNER livery, descending from Burnmouth to Berwick-upon-Tweed with an up express on 25 August 1947. *E. R. Wethersett*

Left:
By now renumbered 60521 and with 'West Riding' headboard in place, *Watling Street* backs out of King's Cross to head for 'Top Shed' in September 1951. It was unusual to have a Gateshead Pacific working this train. *P. Ransome-Wallis*

Below:
Watling Street heads north past York shed with a down express in April 1956. *P. Ransome-Wallis*

60521 *Watling Street*	
Built	Doncaster
Into traffic	8 May 1947 as No 521
Renumbered	60521, 21 May 1948
Allocations	Gateshead, 8 May 1947
	Heaton, 22 May 1960
	Tweedmouth, 1 October 1961
Withdrawn	12 November 1962; to Doncaster Works for scrap, 10 May 1963

Above:
Watling Street accelerates hard over Werrington water troughs before tackling the long climb to Stoke Summit, some 20 miles away, with a down Newcastle express on 22 July 1959. *D. C. Ovenden*

Below:
Having taken the route via Arthington from Harrogate with a Newcastle–Liverpool express, *Watling Street* makes a cautious approach to Leeds City, where it would hand over to ex-LMS power, on 28 May 1960. This locomotive accumulated one of the higher mileages for the class, totalling 836,461 miles in 15½ years (average 53,900 per annum). *Gavin Morrison*

60522 *Straight Deal*

Left:
No 522 *Straight Deal* was one of the few 'A2/3s' to gain an 'E' prefix to its LNER number, as an interim measure following nationalisation. Having adopted its ultimate BR identity of 60522, the locomotive calls at Abbots Ripton on its way south with a Peterborough–King's Cross stopping service on 21 July 1951. *B. S. Jennings*

Below:
Without a trace of exhaust *Straight Deal* heads the 13-coach down 'Heart of Midlothian' as it approaches Potters Bar on 16 July 1955. *Brian Morrison*

Bottom left:
Straight Deal stands outside Doncaster shed on 20 March 1960, following a five-week works visit for general overhaul. *Gavin Morrison*

Right:
Another view of *Straight Deal* on Doncaster shed, this time on 17 June 1962, after its next (and final) general overhaul, which took six weeks. (It would, however, pay 'The Plant' one more visit, towards the end of 1964, for a casual light repair.) Being so recently ex-works it would be transferred to Scotland, notionally in exchange for Scottish 'A2s' transferred (on paper) to the North Eastern Region, in December 1962. *Gavin Morrison*

Below:
Straight Deal's duties at St Margarets mainly involved freight workings, the locomotive being seen leaving Motherwell down yard on 24 July 1963. Two months later it would move to Polmadie, where it did little work and was ultimately withdrawn. *W. S. Sellar*

60522 *Straight Deal*	
Built	Doncaster
Into traffic	19 June 1947 as No 522
Renumbered	E522, 12 February 1948
	60522, 24 September 1949
Allocations	Gateshead, 19 June 1947
	York, 16 August 1947
	Neville Hill, Leeds, 18 January 1948
	York, 30 May 1948
	Aberdeen Ferryhill, 21 December 1962
	St Margarets, 31 December 1962
	Polmadie, 15 September 1963
Withdrawn	19 June 1965; sold to Motherwell Machinery & Scrap Co, July 1965

60523 Sun Castle

Left:
In February 1948, when five months old, No 523 *Sun Castle* prepares to leave Platform 10 at King's Cross with the down 'Flying Scotsman' (10.0am to Edinburgh Waverley), demonstrating that the King's Cross 'A2s' were used on the top jobs alongside the 'A3s' and 'A4s'.
C. C. B. Herbert /
Rail Archive Stephenson

Below:
BR Brunswick green livery was applied to the 'A2/3s' in 1949 and 1950, *Sun Castle* being the first to receive this, after its first general overhaul in July, at which time it also gained its BR identity of 60523. It emerged from the works without the BR emblem on the tender, as shown in this photograph of the locomotive being turned in King's Cross yard on 23 September 1950. *Ian Allan Library*

60523 Sun Castle

Built	Doncaster
Into traffic	2 August 1947 as No 523
Renumbered	60523, 14 July 1949
Allocations	King's Cross, 2 August 1947
	Copley Hill, Leeds, 30 May 1948
	New England, 5 December 1948
	Grantham, 14 December 1958
	New England, 12 April 1959
	Doncaster, 10 January 1960
	New England, 23 September 1962
Withdrawn	16 June 1963; to Doncaster Works for scrap, 28 August 1963

Above:
New England shed must have had some good cleaners in 1958, given the immaculate turn-out of *Sun Castle* at the head of a King's Cross–Newcastle express approaching Stoke Tunnel on 11 September. *T. G. Hepburn / Rail Archive Stephenson*

Below:
Against a backdrop of 'The Plant' *Sun Castle* pulls out of Doncaster with an up express on 29 April 1962. On the right can be seen the standby locomotive ('Thunderbird' in modern parlance), which was a local 'A1'. One of the works 'J50s' can be seen in the background, as can a brand-new AC electric locomotive, while a 'Deltic' diesel-electric can just be discerned standing in the station. *Gavin Morrison*

60524 Herringbone

Left:
The last 'pure' Thompson Pacific, No 524 *Herringbone* entered traffic in apple green in September 1947. Renumbered 60524 and repainted in Brunswick green, it is seen preparing to leave King's Cross with a down express on 20 April 1953. *R. O. Tuck / Rail Archive Stephenson*

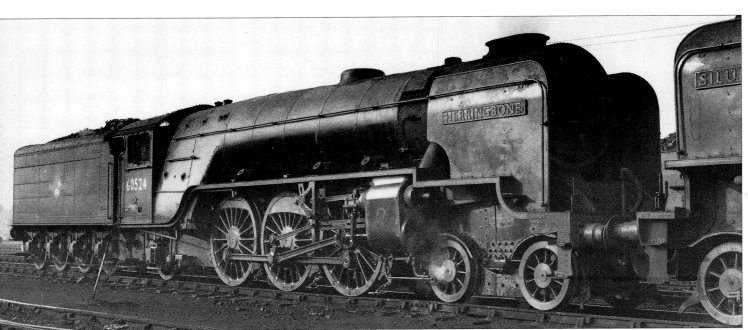

Above:
Herringbone spent most of its working life allocated to York, where it is seen in the shed yard awaiting its next duty on 1 March 1959. *Gavin Morrison*

Left:
Sunday engineering diversions see *Herringbone* passing the distinctive signalbox at Penshaw North on the Leamside line with the up 10.20 Newcastle–King's Cross on 19 July 1959. *I. S. Carr*

Right:
Herringbone spent nine months at Aberdeen Ferryhill, where it shared duties with the 'A4' allocation and 'A3' No 60042 *Singapore*, working the three-hour expresses to/from Glasgow Buchanan Street. On 26 April 1963, however, it was diagrammed for the up postal, being seen near Cove Bay.
D. M. C. Hepburne-Scott / Rail Archive Stephenson

60524 *Herringbone*

Built	Doncaster
Into traffic	26 September 1947 as No 524
Renumbered	60524, 26 January 1949
Allocations	York, 26 September 1947
	Neville Hill, Leeds, 18 January 1948
	York, 26 September 1949
	St Margarets, 2 December 1962
	Aberdeen Ferryhill, 31 December 1962
	Polmadie, 15 September 1963
Withdrawn	15 February 1965; sold to Motherwell Machinery & Scrap Co, May 1965

Right:
Herringbone leaving Perth with the 2.5pm Glasgow Buchanan Street–Aberdeen in June 1963.
P. J. Robinson

Left:
In September 1963 *Herringbone* moved to Polmadie shed (66A) in Glasgow, where there was little work for it. On the night of 9 November it was allocated to a Carlisle–Perth parcels train, being seen at Motherwell. *N. Pollock*

60525 *A. H. Peppercorn*

Above:
The last 15 Thompson standard Pacifics were completed to a design modified by A. H. Peppercorn, being classified as simply 'A2'. Only No 525 *A. H. Peppercorn* entered traffic in LNER days, and only this locomotive and No 526 were given 'L N E R' lettering on the tender. Still so adorned nearly five months after nationalisation, against a backdrop of the massive King's Cross signalbox, No 525 prepares to depart with the 6.5pm to Leeds Central on 13 May 1948. Note the sheet between cab roof and tender. *E. R. Wethersett*

Centre left:
A fine portrait of *A. H. Peppercorn* (by now renumbered 60525) at its home shed of Aberdeen Ferryhill on 8 July 1955. The locomotive was seldom seen south of Edinburgh save when *en route* to or from Doncaster Works, where it received seven general repairs during its brief (15-year) career. *D. Marriott*

Left:
In fine condition, *A. H. Peppercorn* prepares to leave Edinburgh Waverley on 26 May 1957 with a northbound express, which, judging by the sunlight, was probably the late-afternoon departure for Aberdeen, around 5pm. *G. M. Staddon / N. Stead collection*

60525 A. H. Peppercorn	
Built	Doncaster
Into traffic	24 December 1947 as No 525
Renumbered	60525, 25 August 1948
Allocations	Doncaster, 24 December 1947
	New England, 12 December 1948
	Aberdeen Ferryhill, 28 August 1949
Withdrawn	27 March 1963; allocated to St Rollox
	Works for scrap, April 1963,
	but towed to Doncaster

Right:
A classic W. J. V. Anderson photograph, depicting
A. H. Peppercorn emerging from Moncrieff Tunnel at
Hilton Junction, south of Perth, at the head of the 9.30
Aberdeen–Glasgow Buchanan Street in September 1960.
W. J. V. Anderson / Rail Archive Stephenson

Centre right:
A powerful picture of
A. H. Peppercorn getting away from
Perth in fine style, this time taken
at the north end of Moncrieff Tunnel
but again with the 9.30
Aberdeen–Glasgow Buchanan Street,
in April 1961. *W. J. V. Anderson /
Rail Archive Stephenson*

Below:
A. H. Peppercorn at the end of its brief
career of just over 15 years, at
Doncaster Works for scrapping
on 5 May 1963. It is on record that
the locomotive entered St Rollox
Works for scrapping on 14 April
1963. That obviously did not happen
and it must have been towed to
Doncaster. *Gavin Morrison*

60526 *Sugar Palm*

Left:
No 526 *Sugar Palm* was only five months old when this fine picture of it heading a down express was taken near Parkgate Junction, Darlington, in May 1948. Aside from No 525 this was the only 'A2' to emerge from Doncaster Works with 'L N E R' lettering on its apple-green livery, as seen here.
W. Rogerson / Rail Archive Stephenson

Right:
This picture of *Sugar Palm* leaving Newcastle is undated but must have been taken between August 1949, when the locomotive acquired a front numberplate during light repairs, and October of the same year, when BR Brunswick green was applied.
Note the number on the front buffer-beam has been painted out, although the allocation (York) can still be seen. 'BRITISH RAILWAYS' is now painted on the tender. *Ian Allan Library*

Left:
During a general repair at Doncaster in September 1949 *Sugar Palm* was fitted with a multi-valve regulator and double chimney. This fine picture shows the locomotive in this condition heading a Newcastle–Liverpool express near Copmanthorpe, York, on 24 July 1950. It would spend virtually its entire 14-year career working from York shed, prior to being placed in store on 16 September 1962 at Scarborough, where it would ultimately be condemned, having covered 718,432 miles. *C. Ord*

60526 *Sugar Palm*

Built	Doncaster
Into traffic	9 January 1948 as No 526
Renumbered	60526, 26 August 1948
Allocations	York, 9 January 1948
	Neville Hill, Leeds, 18 January 1948
	York, 26 September 1948
Withdrawn	12 November 1962; to Doncaster Works for scrap, 4 April 1963

Above:
Sugar Palm has reached the summit of Stoke Bank as it heads north into Stoke Tunnel with a King's Cross–Newcastle express on 21 July 1962. *Gavin Morrison*

Right:
In excellent condition and with coal piled high in the tender, *Sugar Palm* awaits its next duty at York shed; this may have been some time being assigned, as most workings for York's Pacifics had by now — 1 July 1962 — been turned over to diesel haulage. Three months later it would go into store at Scarborough, finally being condemned on 12 November. *Gavin Morrison*

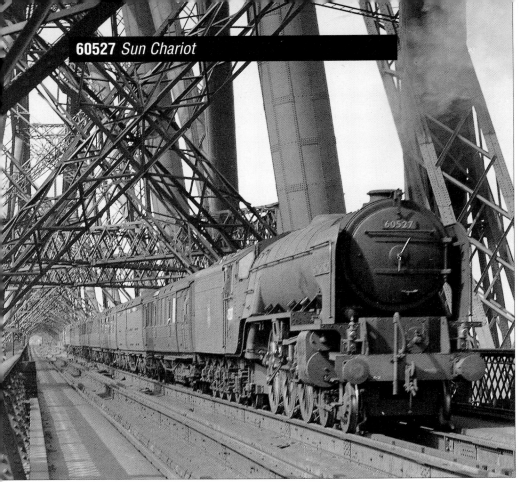

60527 *Sun Chariot*

Left:
Sun Chariot entered service with an 'E' prefix to its LNER-allocated number (as did other 'A2s' up to and including No E531 *Bahram*), as E527. It is pictured on 10 August 1949 heading over the Forth Bridge with an up express, no doubt an Aberdeen–Edinburgh train, which it would have taken over at Dundee. Note the shed allocation still on the buffer-beam. *E. R. Wethersett*

Below:
A fine study of *Sun Chariot*, now with 62B (Dundee) shedplate, heading an up fish train from Aberdeen on 8 June 1951. The train is climbing the 1-in-70 gradient towards North Queensferry at about 20mph, just before entering the tunnel. *E. D. Bruton*

Right:
Sun Chariot leaves Perth in fine style at the head of the 5.30pm Glasgow Buchanan Street–Aberdeen during the summer of 1961. *W. J. V. Anderson / Rail Archive Stephenson*

60527 Sun Chariot

Built	Doncaster
Into traffic	30 January 1948 as No e527
Renumbered	60527, 2 June 1948
Allocations	Gateshead, 30 January 1948
	Dundee, 26 June 1949
	Perth, 4 April 1960
	Aberdeen Ferryhill, 28 May 1960
	Polmadie, 15 September 1963
Withdrawn	24 April 1965; sold to Motherwell
	Machinery & Scrap Co, June 1965

Right:
On 28 March 1964 *Sun Chariot* was allocated to work an RCTS railtour from Glasgow to Aberdeen and is seen putting up a fine exhaust in dismal conditions as it climbs the 1-in-41 Cowlairs Bank. Close examination reveals that, despite a load of just five coaches, it was receiving banking assistance from a North British Type 2 diesel, which in those days was of little interest to your author. How times have changed!
Gavin Morrison

Left:
Jumping into his trusty Volkswagen Beetle, the photographer had no difficulty in reaching Dundee Esplanade station before *Sun Chariot* appeared, drifting down the 1-in-74 gradient from the Tay Bridge. Although the station had closed to passengers on 2 October 1939 the platforms and buildings were intact, and there was no problem with access. *Gavin Morrison*

Left:
After the special had traversed the line up to Kingsmuir behind 'J37' 0-6-0 No 64618, *Sun Chariot* took over again at Broughty Ferry for the return leg to Aberdeen. Despite some spirited driving the photographer only managed to reach Aberdeen at the same time as the train, and without a single picture *en route*. Note the 66A shedplate, indicating that the locomotive was now allocated to Polmadie, although it was little used, and the LMS men there clearly did not regard the 'A2s' as a good exchange for their beloved 'Princess Coronations'. *Gavin Morrison*

Left:
Journey's end for the special. *Sun Chariot*, still with plenty of coal in its tender, awaits removal of the stock at Aberdeen station before heading for Ferryhill shed. *Gavin Morrison*

Right:
No 60528 *Tudor Minstrel* rounds the curve before Chaloners Whin Junction, York, with a down express on 10 July 1948, during its initial 16-month allocation to Gateshead. The combination of apple-green locomotive and teak coaching stock must have made a fine sight.
Tudor Minstrel is nevertheless always associated with the Aberdeen–Edinburgh route, on which it was to spend the majority of its working life.
E. R. Wethersett

Right:
Transferred to Scotland, *Tudor Minstrel* stands at the head of the 9.50 Aberdeen–Edinburgh Waverley express, preparing to leave the Granite City on 31 July 1953. Being a Dundee engine, it would be exchanged there for a Haymarket Pacific. *Brian Morrison*

60528 *Tudor Minstrel*

Built	Doncaster
Into traffic	21 February 1948 as No E528
Renumbered	60528, 25 June 1948
Allocations	Gateshead, 21 February 1948
	Dundee, 26 June 1949
	Perth, 2 May 1950
	Aberdeen Ferryhill, 28 May 1960
	Dundee, 19 June 1961
	Aberdeen Ferryhill, 24 April 1966
Withdrawn	2 June 1966; sold for scrap to J. McWilliam, Shettleston, August 1966

Right:
No date is available for this picture of *Tudor Minstrel* crossing the Forth Bridge on an express, but it must have been taken after the previous one, as the numberplate is now in the lower position. The man working on the bridge, very close to the passing train, hasn't even bothered to look up.
Ian Allan Library

Left:
In fine condition, *Tudor Minstrel* awaits its next duty at Dundee Tay Bridge shed on 8 June 1957. *Gavin Morrison*

Below left:
Tudor Minstrel seems to be having no difficulty in hauling the Aberdeen–Edinburgh Waverley up the 1-in-70 gradient from Inverkeithing as it leaves the tunnel at North Queensferry before heading across the Forth Bridge on 22 August 1959. *D. T. Greenwood / Rail Archive Stephenson*

Above right:
The fine signal gantry at the south end of Stirling station provides a backdrop to *Tudor Minstrel* as the 'A2' heads south with a Dundee–Glasgow Buchanan Street express *c*1960. *W. J. V. Anderson / Rail Archive Stephenson*

Centre right:
In the company of King's Cross 'A4' No 60007 *Sir Nigel Gresley*, *Tudor Minstrel* stands dead on the 'awaiting works' road at Doncaster shed on 29 April 1962. This was the occasion of its last general repair, the locomotive being out of service for about 11 weeks. *Gavin Morrison*

Right:
Another fine study of *Tudor Minstrel*, this time at Dundee Tay Bridge shed, where it was allocated for 11 years. Seen on 5 June 1965, the locomotive had only a year of service before withdrawal. *M. S. Welch*

Left:
In June 1954, when Haymarket's locomotives were all kept in immaculate condition, *Pearl Diver* pulls out of Edinburgh Waverley at the head of the up 'Heart of Midlothian'; note the headboard is in the lower position. This was the only Haymarket 'A2' to receive the double chimney and multiple-valve regulator (the other Scottish 'A2' so fitted being *Blue Peter*, allocated to Dundee and Aberdeen Ferryhill), on which grounds it was considered superior to the single-chimney examples. *J. Robertson*

60529 *Pearl Diver*	
Built	Doncaster
Into traffic	21 February 1948 as No E529
Renumbered	60529, 16 September 1949
Allocations	Haymarket, 21 February 1948
	St Margarets, 16 October 1961
Withdrawn	29 December 1962; sold for scrap to
	G. H. Campbell, Airdrie, June 1964

Left:
Pearl Diver spent all its working days allocated to the Edinburgh sheds. This fine study was recorded at Edinburgh Waverley station on 31 July 1953. The locomotive had just arrived with the 9.50 from Aberdeen, which it had taken over at Dundee. *Brian Morrison*

Left:
The following day *Pearl Diver* was busy on another up express, seen near Dunfermline. *Brian Morrison*

Above:
Gateshead was the furthest south one was likely to see a Haymarket 'A2' in normal service, unless it was on its way to or from Doncaster Works. Awaiting its return to Edinburgh, *Pearl Diver* stands outside the shed on 26 August 1954. *Brian Morrison*

Centre right:
By 4 April 1959 *Pearl Diver* had received a cast-iron chimney, which most consider improved its appearance. Seen near Carlisle Kingmoor shed, the four-coach 3.22pm Carlisle–Edinburgh Waverley stopper was easy work for a powerful Pacific. *R. Leslie*

Right:
Like many Haymarket Pacifics *Pearl Diver* was dumped at Bathgate following withdrawal at the end of 1962, and this picture, taken there on 2 June 1963 presents a sorry sight. The once-proud 'A2' would linger for a further year before disposal to G. H. Campbell of Airdrie for scrapping.
Gavin Morrison

Left:
Sayajirao was only around six weeks old when this fine portrait was taken on the turntable at Grantham, where it had been turned to head south to its then home shed of King's Cross, on 24 April 1948. Its temporary number (E530) can be clearly seen on the apple-green livery.
J. P. Wilson / Rail Archive Stephenson

Right:
Another fine picture of *Sayajirao*, still with its 'E' number, this time seen heading the 1.10pm King's Cross–Leeds Central at Lofthouse (near Wakefield) on 13 August 1948.
E. R. Wethersett

Left:
Renumbered 60530 and transferred to Scotland, *Sayajirao* was badly damaged in the Longniddry accident of December 1953 but is seen here in the immaculate condition typical of Haymarket locomotives the mid-1950s, passing through Princes Street Gardens, Edinburgh, with the 2.15pm from Waverley to Aberdeen on 28 March 1957. On the right is the equally well turned-out Waverley pilot, ex-North British Class J83 0-6-0T No 68481. *G. M. Staddon / N. Stead collection*

Above:
Few pictures seem to have been taken in steam days at Glasgow Queen Street High Level (and even fewer at the lower level), but *Sayajirao* was caught at the buffer-stops with a parcels train on 13 May 1961.
M. Mensing

Right:
Having arrived via the Waverley route, *Sayajirao* simmers at Carlisle Canal shed awaiting its next duty back to Edinburgh on 6 April 1963, the year the shed closed. *Gavin Morrison*

60530 *Sayajirao*

Built	Doncaster
Into traffic	4 March 1948 as No E530
Renumbered	60530, 17 November 1949
Allocations	King's Cross, 4 March 1948
	New England, 12 December 1948
	Haymarket, 9 January 1950
	St Margarets, 16 October 1961
	Polmadie, 15 September 1963
	Dundee, 31 July 1964
Withdrawn	19 November 1966; sold to Motherwell Machinery & Scrap Co, March 1967

Right:
The gloomy conditions of Edinburgh's St Margarets shed are well shown in this picture of *Sayajirao* steaming in the yard on 15 April 1966. The local residents must have been delighted when the shed closed in 1967, as the atmosphere (especially on a Sunday night, when locomotives were being steamed from cold in preparation for service the following day) was absolutely terrible. It was also an extremely dangerous place, as it was very congested and the offices were on the opposite side of the main line, with virtually no warning of up trains. *W. B. Alexander*

Left:
Bahram was the last 'A2' to enter traffic with an 'ᴇ' prefix to its originally intended LNER number, in March 1948, assuming its BR identity as 60531 later in the year. After a five-week general overhaul, the locomotive stands in Doncaster Works yard, ready to return to its home shed of Aberdeen Ferryhill, on 13 November 1955.
Gavin Morrison

Below:
Caley 'Jumbo' No 57253, fresh from overhaul at Inverurie Works, backs off Aberdeen Ferryhill shed as *Bahram* storms by with the 5.17pm express from the Granite City to Edinburgh Waverley on 25 June 1957. *Brian Morrison*

60531 *Bahram*

Built	Doncaster
Into traffic	12 March 1948 as No ᴇ531
Renumbered	60531, 25 November 1948
Allocations	Gateshead, 12 March 1948
	Aberdeen Ferryhill, 7 August 1949
	York, 2 December 1962
	('paper' transfer only)
Withdrawn	10 December 1962;
	to Doncaster Works for scrap

Above:
After climbing the seven miles out of Aberdeen, *Bahram* passes along the cliffs by the North Sea near Cove Bay with a morning Aberdeen–Edinburgh Waverley express in the late 1950s. *W. J. V. Anderson / Rail Archive Stephenson*

Below:
Unfortunately there are no details to accompany this fine study of *Bahram*, seen probably at Doncaster shed after its last general overhaul in December 1960. *Ian Allan Library*

60532 Blue Peter

Built	Doncaster
Into traffic	25 March 1948 as No 60532
Allocations	York, 25 March 1948
	Haymarket, 27 November 1949
	Aberdeen Ferryhill, 7 January 1951
	Dundee, 19 June 1961
	Aberdeen Ferryhill, 4 December 1966
Withdrawn	31 December 1966; sold for preservation, 21 August 1968

Right:
No 60532 *Blue Peter* was the first 'A2' to enter traffic with its BR number. Obviously ex works, it is seen just south of Grantham with an up freight on 8 September 1951. Having just been released from Doncaster after a casual light repair due to a derailment, it was probably working this train as a running-in turn before returning to Aberdeen. Its multi-valve regulator and double chimney were fitted in September 1949. *T. G. Hepburn / Rail Archive Stephenson*

Right:
Blue Peter was the only 'A2' fitted with a double chimney and a multi-valve regulator to be based for any length of time at Aberdeen Ferryhill, where it is said to have been a better performer than the single-chimney members on the difficult Aberdeen–Dundee–Edinburgh route. The locomotive is seen hauling the heavy night 'Aberdonian' out of the Granite City near Ferryhill on 25 June 1957. *Brian Morrison*

Left:
By May 1966 the remaining Scottish 'A2s' had little work. Here *Blue Peter* and *Sayajirao* await the next call of duty at Dundee Tay Bridge shed on 28 May 1966. The picture facilitates comparison between single- and double-chimney locomotives. *M. Welch*

Right:
Probably the furthest *Blue Peter* ever wandered away from its East Coast duties in BR ownership was when it was called upon to haul the 'Brymbo Special' from Manchester Central to Holyhead on 21 August 1966. On a very wet morning it is shown preparing to leave Manchester Central, which would close on 5 May 1969.
Gavin Morrison

Below:
Blue Peter obviously returned from its North Wales trip all right, as by 31 August 1966 it was back on its normal duties, being seen ready to leave Glasgow Buchanan Street with the 11.30pm to Perth and Aberdeen.
L. A. Nixon

60533 *Happy Knight*

Built	Doncaster
Into traffic	9 April 1948 as No 60533
Allocations	New England, 9 April 1948
	Copley Hill, Leeds, 29 May 1948
	New England, 19 December 1948
	Copley Hill, Leeds, 12 March 1950
	New England, 30 April 1950
	Annesley, 2 July 1950
	New England, 9 July 1950
	Grantham, 20 June 1954
	New England, 16 September 1956
	Grantham, 15 September 1957
	King's Cross, 8 June 1958
	Grantham, 14 December 1958
	New England, 14 June 1959
	Doncaster, 10 January 1960
	New England, 23 September 1962
Withdrawn	15 June 1963; to Doncaster Works for scrap, 2 September 1963

Above:
Happy Knight heads out of King's Cross and climbs Holloway Bank, probably heading for Leeds, on 27 May 1948, during its first spell (of seven!) allocated to New England shed. *E. R. Wethersett*

Below:
With its single chimney, in apple-green livery and with the 'Yorkshire Pullman' behind it, No 60533 *Happy Knight* must have made a very impressive sight entering King's Cross at the end of its journey from Leeds Central sometime in the summer or autumn of 1948, judging from the 'COPLEY HILL' allocation on the buffer-beam. *C. R. L. Cotes / Rail Archive Stephenson*

Right:
Fitted with a multi-valve regulator and double chimney during a general repair in December 1949, *Happy Knight* was unique among 'A2s' in being based to Annesley shed on the Great Central section, albeit for just one week, in July 1950. This picture shows the locomotive about to enter Copenhagen Tunnel near the end of its journey from Peterborough to King's Cross on 29 June 1953, by which time its allocation had reverted to New England. *Brian Morrison*

Right:
In the early 1960s the Doncaster-allocated Pacifics were often used on Leeds Central–Doncaster stopping trains. A three-coach load presents no problem for *Happy Knight* as it pulls out of Wakefield Westgate at the head of the 2.5pm from Leeds on 19 July 1961. The long-since-demolished station clock tower can be seen in the background. *Gavin Morrison*

Right:
For its last nine months of service *Happy Knight* moved to New England, where it had little work — and little attention, at least externally. It is seen in front of a 'V2' at Doncaster shed on 19 May 1963. *Gavin Morrison*

60534 *Irish Elegance*

60534 *Irish Elegance*

Left:
Without a trace of exhaust, No 60534 *Irish Elegance* climbs to the summit of Glenfarg past Mawcarse Junction on the now closed line to Perth with the 4.5pm express from Edinburgh Waverley in the summer of 1955.
W. J. V. Anderson / Rail Archive Stephenson

Below left:
Fresh from general overhaul at 'The Plant', *Irish Elegance* stands outside Doncaster shed on 14 July 1959. It would receive its last general overhaul in February 1961.
G. Wheeler

60534 *Irish Elegance*

Built	Doncaster
Into traffic	23 April 1948 as No 60534
Allocations	York, 23 April 1948
	Haymarket, 27 November 1949
	St Margarets, 13 November 1961
Withdrawn	29 December 1962; sold for scrap to
	G. H. Campbell, Airdrie, June 1964

Below:
The depressing sight of *Irish Elegance*, awaiting disposal to G. H. Campbell of Airdrie for scrapping, dumped at Bathgate shed on 2 June 1963. *Gavin Morrison*

Above:
For its last year of service *Irish Elegance* was transferred to Edinburgh's St Margarets shed, where the attention afforded it at Haymarket was sadly lacking. It is seen on 12 April 1962 in the company of Gateshead 'A3' No 60052 *Prince Palatine* at the very unusual (for an 'A2') location of Leeds Holbeck shed, having worked south during the night with the Edinburgh Waverley–London St Pancras sleeper, in place of a failed 'Peak' Type 4 diesel. Note the change of dome from that seen in the previous picture. *Gavin Morrison*

60535 *Hornets Beauty*

Built	Doncaster
Into traffic	5 May 1948 as No 60535
Allocations	York, 5 May 1948
	Haymarket, 27 November 1949
	St Margarets, 16 October 1961
	Polmadie, 15 September 1963
Withdrawn	19 June 1965; to Motherwell
	Machinery & Scrap Co, July 1965

Left:
A fine study of No 60535 *Hornets Beauty* in apple green at York, when new in 1948. *Eric Treacy*

Below left:
The winter of 1962/3 was very severe, as is readily apparent from this picture of *Hornets Beauty* well and truly stuck in the drifts between Whitrope and Riccarton Junction in January 1963. One wonders how the photographer managed to get to this remote location; maybe he was part of the snow-clearing operation. *P. Brock*

Above right:
Hornets Beauty was one of the 'A2s' transferred to Glasgow's Polmadie shed to replace ex-LMS 'Princess Coronations' — a move not appreciated by the Polmadie crews. By June 1964 there was little work for them; on the 24th *Hornets Beauty* was diagrammed for the all-stations Glasgow–Carlisle, seen arriving at Beattock and passing the shed (left). *T. G. Hepburn / Rail Archive Stephenson*

Centre right:
Hornets Beauty, now with yellow cabside stripe barring it from working under the wires south of Crewe, stands on the turntable at the south end of Carlisle Kingmoor shed, being turned prior to returning to Kingmoor yard to work a down freight, on 26 September 1964. *Gavin Morrison*

Right:
Two weeks before its official withdrawal, *Hornets Beauty* stands stored out of use at the back of Polmadie shed in Glasgow. In the background is No 60527 *Sun Chariot*, which had been withdrawn two months earlier. Between February 1956 and November 1957 *Hornets Beauty* had recorded the highest mileage between general repairs of any 'A2', covering 127,830 miles. *M. S. Welch*

60536 *Trimbush*

Built	Doncaster
Into traffic	14 May 1948 as No 60536
Allocations	Copley Hill, Leeds, 14 May 1948
	New England, 26 December 1948
	Haymarket, 20 November 1949
	St Margarets, 13 November 1961
	Haymarket, 14 May 1962
	St Margarets, 8 October 1962
	York, 2 December 1962
	('paper' transfer only)
Withdrawn	17 December 1962; to Doncaster Works
	for scrap

Right:
Trimbush hurries along the relatively level section of line near Prestonpans at the head of the 9.10am Glasgow Queen Street–Newcastle on 20 June 1952. *E. R. Wethersett*

Below:
In dismal conditions No 60536 *Trimbush* gets a push from a Class N15 0-6-2T banker as it approaches the summit of the 1-in-41 Cowlairs Bank with the 11am from Glasgow Queen Street to Edinburgh Waverley on 13 July 1956. *Gavin Morrison*

Above:
Trimbush makes a fine picture as it passes under a bridge approaching Penmanshiel Tunnel with the 10.15 Edinburgh–Newcastle on 5 May 1959. The tunnel would collapse in 1979, resulting in tragic loss of life, and was never reopened, a diversion being built to replace it. *H. Harman*

Right:
In December 1962 *Trimbush* was transferred 'on paper' to York but never actually arrived. However, it was definitely present five months before withdrawal, being seen over the ashpits on 1 July 1962. Despite its terrible external condition, its electric lighting is still fitted. *Gavin Morrison*

60537 Bachelors Button

Built	Doncaster
Into traffic	11 June 1948 as No 60537
Allocations	Copley Hill, Leeds, 11 June 1948
	New England, 2 January 1949
	Aberdeen Ferryhill, 1 July 1949
	Haymarket, 7 January 1951
	St Margarets, 13 November 1961
Withdrawn	29 December 1962; sold for scrap
	to Henderson's of Airdrie, June 1964

Left:
Nos 60534-9 appeared new with cast-iron numberplates fitted on the smokebox door. When just a few weeks old, No 60537 *Bachelors Button* stands on the turntable in King's Cross yard, with Gasworks Tunnel on the right. The picture shows the larger cabside numbers, as applied to Nos 60532-8. *Ian Allan Library*

Above:
Although not up to Haymarket's usual high standard of presentation, *Bachelors Button* still makes an impressive sight at the head of the up 'Queen of Scots', passing Manuel (between Polmont and Linlithgow) on 30 October 1954. *W. J. V. Anderson / Rail Archive Stephenson*

Above:
A powerful picture of *Bachelors Button* as it pulls away from Longtown with the 2.36pm Edinburgh Waverley–Carlisle stopper on 16 April 1960. *R. Leslie*

Below:
Still with electric lights fitted but by now devoid of nameplates, *Bachelors Button* stands in Bathgate shed yard on 31 March 1964, awaiting its final journey to Henderson's of Airdrie for scrapping. *Gavin Morrison*

60538 *Velocity*

Left:
With its allocation ('G'HEAD') clearly visible on the buffer-beam, No 60538 *Velocity* stands over the ashpits at York shed on 13 September 1948, when three months old. *B. G. Tweed / N. Stead collection*

Below:
With a liberal coating of grime obscuring its lovely apple-green paint, *Velocity* heads the up 'Flying Scotsman' towards Peascliffe Tunnel on 6 August 1949. A month later the 'A2' would disappear into Doncaster Works, emerging with a double chimney and multiple-valve regulator. *T. G. Hepburn / Rail Archive Stephenson*

60538 *Velocity*

Built	Doncaster
Into traffic	18 June 1948 as No 60538
Allocations	Gateshead, 18 June 1948
	Heaton, 22 May 1960
	Tweedmouth, 1 October 1961
Withdrawn	12 November 1962; to Doncaster Works for scrap, 13 May 1963

Above:
Now with its double chimney, *Velocity* enters York at the head of an up cross-country express in the early 1950s.
N. Stead collection

Right:
A striking backlit shot of *Velocity* heading north out of Berwick-upon-Tweed with a down freight at 9pm on 30 May 1962. The 'A2s' did not achieve high mileages during their brief careers, although *Velocity* probably managed the highest total by the end of 1962, its 890,627 miles giving an annual average of around 63,500.
M. Mensing

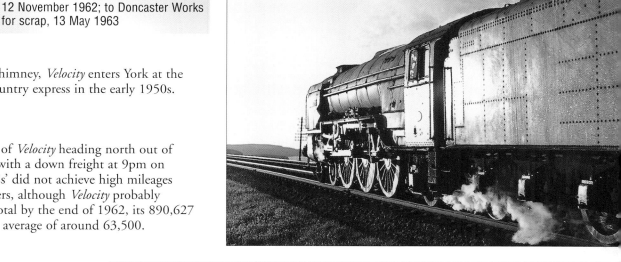

Right:
Velocity entered Doncaster Works for cutting-up on 13 May 1963. One week later it was still in one piece but would not be for much longer. Alongside are a withdrawn King's Cross 'A4' — No 60013 *Dominion of New Zealand* — and, in sharp contrast, clean EE Type 3 and Brush Type 2 diesels. *Gavin Morrison*

Above:
No 60539 *Bronzino* was the last 'A2' to be built and the only one fitted from new with the Kylchap double blastpipe and chimney. Still in apple green with 'BRITISH RAILWAYS' on the tender, and clearly proclaiming its allocation to Heaton, the locomotive is pictured at Grantham shed on 7 May 1949.
J. P. Wilson / Rail Archive Stephenson

60539 *Bronzino*	
Built	Doncaster
Into traffic	27 August 1948 as No 60539
Allocations	Heaton, 27 August 1948
	Tweedmouth, 1 October 1961
Withdrawn	12 November 1962; to Doncaster Works for scrap, 19 April 1963

Left:
For almost its entire career *Bronzino* was the sole representative of the double-chimney 'A2' at Heaton shed; it also differed from the other five double-chimney 'A2s' in not being fitted with a multi-valve regulator. On 25 July 1952 the locomotive was photographed working a down express near the English/Scottish border. *E. R. Wethersett*

Right:
Passing beneath the very impressive signal gantry at the south end of the station, *Bronzino* arrives at Newcastle with an express from King's Cross on 16 June 1953. It is likely that it had taken over from a King's Cross Pacific at Grantham. By this date the locomotive was roughly halfway between general repairs, which were only 15 months apart, so it must have been clocking up high mileages around this time. *R. Leslie*

Centre right:
Now running with cast-iron chimney, *Bronzino* enjoys a taste of top-link work as it passes Selby with an up express on 23 May 1959. The very high signals would have been visible to drivers from the swing bridge at the north end of the station.
Brian Morrison

Below:
A fine panned shot of *Bronzino* hurrying down the bank towards Berwick-upon-Tweed, with the North Sea in the background, on 30 May 1962. It spent its last years at Tweedmouth, where there was little work for it, its career ending six months after this picture was taken, by which time it had covered 769,552 miles. *M. Mensing*

'A2' No 60532 *Blue Peter* in Preservation

Left:
Blue Peter leaves the modernised Bradford Forster Square station for Carlisle with an NELPG special on 28 March 1992. *Gavin Morrison*

Below:
The long awaited main-line test run for *Blue Peter* took place on 27 February 1992 between Derby and Sheffield. Despite having 14 coaches in tow it had no difficulty in climbing the 1-in-100 out of Sheffield past Millhouses to Dore & Totley, but unfortunately it failed later at Clay Cross. *Gavin Morrison*

Right:
Prior to its main-line debut *Blue Peter* was used to haul trains on the North Yorkshire Moors Railway, being seen here at Darnholm with the 11.15 Grosmont–Pickering on 30 December 1991. *Brian Dobbs*

Overleaf:
Heading north for a trip over the Settle & Carlisle, *Blue Peter* climbs out of Blackburn and up the bank to Wilpshire on 7 March 1992. This was its first main-line trip in preservation. *Gavin Morrison*

Below:
Blue Peter leaves Stirling for Edinburgh with the 'Aberdonian' special on 17 October 1993. The locomotive saw extensive main-line use during the 1990s but is now (2004) on show at Darlington North Road Museum. *Brian Dobbs*